Praise for

Promise of a Rainbow

"I really enjoyed *Promise of a Rainbow* which surprised me because I'm not a poetry reader at all. What I truly enjoyed were the vignettes that accompanied each poem. I found myself engrossed in those short stories and situations that helped me to appreciate each poem even more. This is a book that every kind of reader will enjoy."

— VICTORIA CHRISTOPHER MURRAY, *ESSENCE* BESTSELLING AUTHOR

"This work is thoughtful and introspective, and challenges the reader to find their own meaning in God's word."

— NINA FOXX, AWARD-WINNING FILMMAKER, PLAYWRIGHT, AND NOVELIST

"Promise of a Rainbow delivers a delightful pathway to understanding His promises."

— VICTOR MCGLOTHIN, BESTSELLING NOVELIST, FILMMAKER AND TV SHOW CREATOR

ALSO BY
PAMELA WALKER-WILLIAMS

In a Heartbeat: A Collection of Poetry

Marian of Memphis
(*A Letter For My Mother* Anthology,
Edited by Nina Fox)

*A Dash of Soul: Recipes and Stories from
the Bluff City of Memphis*

COMING SOON

Spiritual Gifts: A Novel

PROMISE OF A RAINBOW

Compilation Copyright © 1994, 2015 Pamela Walker-Williams
The Page-Turner Network
2951 Marina Bay Dr., Suite 130
League City, TX 77573
www.pageturner.net

All Rights Reserved.
Printed in the United States of America.

No part of this publication by be reprinted, stored in a retrieval system, or transmitted in a form without prior permission of the publisher.

Some of the poems in this collection were published as:

Promises Kept and Broken - 1994

First Edition

10 9 8 7 6 5 4 3 2 1

ISBN-10: 0982890931
ISBN-13: 978-0-9828909-3-6

Layout Designed by: PW2 Design

Cover Illustration by: © artant | Dollar Photo Club
Icon Illustrations by: © Strezhnev Pavel | Dollar Photo Club

Text Edited by: Juanita Cole Towery and Jan Emanuel-Costley

Promise of a Rainbow

PAMELA WALKER-WILLIAMS

STILETTO PRESS IMPRINT

THE PAGE-TURNER NETWORK | TEXAS

2015

Dedication

TO RUFFUS
MY HUSBAND,
MY BEST FRIEND,
MY JOY

But seek ye first the kingdom of God,
And his righteousness;
And all these things shall be added unto you.
Matthew 6:33 (KJV)

Contents

Introduction	9
The Shadow of Wings	17
On My Knees	21
I Sent My Child to School to Learn	27
Secret Snow	33
Economic Bondage	37
Women of the Cross	41
The Call	47
Unto Others	51
Letting Go	55
Dream Dancer	59
The Passing of Youth	63
Sense Me	67
A Silenced Woof	71
The Gift of Thanks	75
Bandwagon	79
Coming Down the Mountain	83
Ancestor Unknown	91
A Dash of Soul	97
My Joy	101
The Broken Promise	105
Promise of a Rainbow	111
Study Guide	115

Introduction

Life is full of promises. Man's promises can be broken, but God's promises are always kept.

Those were the opening words to the 1st edition of the book "Promises Kept and Broken" that I published in 1994. It was a small booklet I prepared for a church event that contained 10 poems with corresponding scriptures that pertained to everyday life.

This tiny booklet became the catalyst igniting my study of God's promises. The results grew into a revised book that is re-titled "Promise of a Rainbow."

For each poem, I started with a single question "What does God have to say about this?" After searching the Bible for the answer, I divided my responses into five categories:

1. Commandments and Instructions
2. Facts and Examples
3. Praise and Prayer
4. Promises
5. Convants

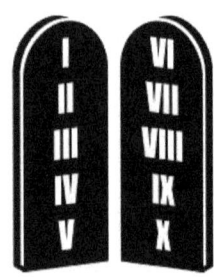
Commandments and Instructions

- Commandment – a divine rule or mandate given by God
- Instruction – directions

Facts and Examples

- Fact – something known to exist or to have happened in the past
- Example (Parable) – a story that illustrates a spiritual or moral lesson

Praise and Prayer

- Praise – the offering of grateful admiration
- Prayer – a spiritual communion with God

Promises
- Promise – a declaration that God will or will not do something in the future; it is unconditional and based on God's Grace

Covenants

- Covenant – a solemn agreement made to humanity by God; a conditional agreement, contains a promise based on a fact or instruction

COMMANDMENTS AND INSTRUCTIONS

- A divine rule or mandate given by God
- Directions

We are all familiar with God's commandments (especially the "big 10"); but these commandments are not all encompassing. In addition to the 10 commandments, God has given us additional laws, rules, and instructions to follow. Following these rules help us meet His expectations of us, for example:

John 13:34 (NIV)
"A new command I give you: Love one another. As I have loved you, so you must love one another."

In this example, Jesus commands us to love one another; and we are given explicit instruction of how it is to be done.

FACTS AND PARABLES

- Fact – something known to exist or to have happened in the past
- Example (Parable) – a story that illustrates a spiritual or moral lesson

In addition to giving us instructions, we can also reference the bible for historical facts, stories with examples, advice, and parables.

For example, the book of Isaiah was written between 701 and 681 B.C. and it contains the fact that the earth is a sphere, which we now know is a fact:

Isaiah 40:22 (NIV)
He sits enthroned above the circle of the earth, and its people are like grasshoppers. He stretches out the heavens like a canopy, and spreads them out like a tent to live in.

PRAISE AND PRAYER

- Praise – the offering of grateful admiration
- Prayer – a spiritual communion with God

Prayer is how we commune with God. Through prayer we ask God to come into our lives, we give thanks for what we have, and we share our joys and struggles with Him.

Through praise we testify to all what God has done for us. The bible teaches us to praise the Lord, and there are many examples of praise and prayer.

Psalm 4:1 (NIV)
Answer me when I call to you, O my righteous God. Give me relief from my distress; be merciful to me and hear my prayer.

Revelation 4:11 (NIV)
You are worthy, our Lord and God, to receive glory and honor and power, for you created all things, and by your will they were created and have their being.

PROMISES

- A declaration that God will or will not do something in the future.

- It is unconditional and based on God's Grace.

The bible is full of God's unconditional promises to us. These are promises that He has made to us without expecting us to do anything in return. These are also examples of God's grace.

Genesis 9:13 (NIV)
I have set my rainbow in the clouds, and it will be the sign of the covenant between me and the earth.

COVENANTS

- A solemn agreement made to humanity by God.
- A conditional agreement, contains a promise based on a fact or instruction.

Not all of God's promises are unconditional. In many cases, God promises that He will do something in the future based on us fulfilling a specific condition. This condition can be an instruction or a fact. For example when you tell your children "If you clean up your room, you can go outside to play." You just made a conditional promise, or a covenant.

> The condition: *If they* clean up their room
> The promise: *You will* allow them to go outside to play.

Just as we make conditional promises to our children, God makes conditional promises to us.

Proverbs 3:6 (KJV)
In all thy ways acknowledge Him and He shall direct thy paths.

This scripture is straight and to the point -

    The Condition: ***If we*** acknowledge God
    The Promise: ***He will*** direct our paths.

I am in not a biblical scholar. There is no exact science to my approach. I write about what I know and what I have experienced, and I have sought God's word to understand it better.

People have been trying to interpret the Bible for centuries; and there are a whole lot of people (who are a lot smarter than I am) who will continue to debate religious doctrine. This book is not a part of that debate.

My prayer is that there is something in these pages that God wants you to know. If so, I am thankful that He chose me to be the one to reveal it to you.

Romans 8:28 (KJV)
And we know that in all things God works for the good of those who love Him, who have been called according to His purpose.

P. WALKER-WILLIAMS

The Shadow of Wings

Sometimes we all see angels
Yet we don't know they are there
They come around to guide us
We don't know when or where.

Sometimes we all hear angels
They whisper in our ears
Speaking softly just to calm us
In the midst of all our fears.

Sometimes we feel their presence
As they gently take our hands
Those times when we feel lonely

The angels understand.
Angels all around us
What a comfort this thought brings
Knowing they'll protect us
In the shadow of their wings.

THE SHADOW OF WINGS

Psalm 17:8 (NIV)
Keep me as the apple of the eye, hide me under the shadow of thy wings.

I have always been fascinated by angels. Such beautiful beings, created by God and mentioned in the bible 273 times! I have prayed to God many times asking him to send His angels to protect my family, my friends and myself. The thought of angels inspired me to write not only this poem, but also my novel Spiritual Gifts. I wrote "The Shadow of Wings" in 1993. The title was taken from the last line of the poem.

The line "Angels all around us, what a comfort this thought brings" was inspired by God's instruction to us:

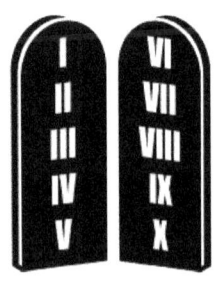

Hebrews 13:2 (NIV)
Do not forget to show hospitality to strangers, for by so doing some people have shown hospitality to angels without knowing it.

There are many times when I am approached by panhandlers or a homeless person that I remind myself this person might be an angel.

Lastly, I searched to see if God made any promise concerning angels, and I found:

Psalm 91:11-12 (NIV)

For he will command His angels concerning you to guard you in all your ways; they will lift you up in their hands, so that you will not strike your foot against a stone.

This is an unconditional promise:

He will command His angels to protect you.

Wow, as the poem says, "What a comfort this thought brings!"

P. WALKER-WILLIAMS

On My Knees

When the day has been long
And you're tired as can be.
After the children do their homework
And they're fed and gone to sleep.
When the house is calm and quiet
And you feel your soul at ease.
It's a perfect time to pray
On your knees.

When you have lost your job
And there's no money to be found
You are down on your luck
Your whole world is upside down.
When you stretch your hand to Jesus
And you ask Him, Father, please!
It is time to talk it over
On your knees.

We can call on the Father
Any time of day
While just driving in the car,
It's the perfect time to pray.
Jesus always listens, and He knows your every need.
But there's a special joy of praying
On your knees.

When I awake in the morning
And as I get out of bed
Before I start my day
There's something to be said.
Father, I'm so grateful
That you watched over me
And I give you all the glory
On my knees.

ON MY KNEES

1 Timothy 2:8 (NIV)
Therefore, I want the men everywhere to pray, lifting up holy hands without anger or disputing.

Prayer works. Although sometimes the results are not what we want or expect, your prayers are always answered. Praying is how we communicate with God; and it is through prayer that we can renew our faith.

When my brother was killed, I was so angry with God. My family and friends all prayed and prayed, but he still died. I thought, even if God was ignoring my prayers, He would surely have answered the prayers of my mother. She was such a better person than I, she was a good and faithful servant. When he died, I truly felt that my prayer was unanswered.

God knew what quality of life my brother would have had if he had survived, so God did answer my prayer, He chose to give my brother eternal life instead. I now know that God knows WAY more than I do (and that is a good thing or we would all be in a world of trouble.)

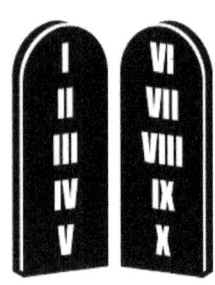

Matthew 6:7 (NIV)
And when you pray, do not keep on babbling like pagans, for they think they will be heard because of their many words.

I often marvel at the way some people pray such eloquent prayers. They use such big and sanctified words. Half the time, I have no idea what they are talking about, but it sounds real holy. Have you ever been at a family gathering and when that "special" family member begins to bless the food they sound as if they are speaking at a presidential inauguration?

Of course, many of these people are sincere in their prayers, but I am sure just as many are babbling and just putting on a grand performance. I have even noticed the difference in myself when someone asks me to pray in public. In public, my prayers are very formal. I try to use the correct nomenclature and all of the church-approved idioms I have heard all of my life. However, when I am praying alone it is more conversational and more from my heart.

Matthew 6:6 (NIV)
But when you pray, go into your room, close the door and pray to your Father, who is unseen. Then your Father, who sees what is done in secret, will reward you.

The Condition: Be sincere when you pray, not just for show.

The Promise: God will reward you.

P. WALKER-WILLIAMS

I Sent My Child to School to Learn

I sent my child to school to learn
To help achieve his dreams
Instead they stole all of his goals
And all his self-esteem.

They all feared the one Black child
who soon would be a man.
So they rushed to rob him now,
The only time they can.

For if you enslave one's mind
You don't need locks or chains
So make him feel inadequate now
And submissive he'll remain.

But they did not count on me
To put a dent into their plan.
I have long been acquainted with racism
And the plot to destroy the Black man.

My child is the descendant of
Kings and Queens
From the cradle of mankind
And education is the key
To unlock and free his mind.

We must provide an atmosphere
That is full of love and concern
So our children can grow
in body and mind
And so they can be free to learn.

So as a mother I take this vow
To my child and to yours
To help knock down the walls of hate
And open up love's doors.

I SENT MY CHILD TO SCHOOL TO LEARN

Isaiah 54:17 (KJV)
No weapon that is formed against thee shall prosper; and every tongue that shall rise against thee in judgment thou shalt condemn…

There is a great deal that has happened to widen the divide in race relations since I wrote this poem in the early 90's. At that time, my son was in grade school and my African-American child was attending a predominately white school. In addition to typical children repeating stupid things they heard their parents say (a.k.a., the n-word), he also had some small-minded teachers who did not always have his best interest in mind. It was during this time when he and I first had "the talk" that has recently been recounted in the aftermath of Trevon Martin and Michael Brown.

In the 4th grade, my son had a teacher publicly call him dumb in class; in intermediate school, his counselors sent a letter to me notifying me that statistics show children from single-parent households probably will not graduate from high school; and in high school (when it was apparent he was going to graduate) he was told he should consider the military because he didn't have college potential (he was a "B" not "A" student.) Thank God, we answer to a higher power and did not let their insensitive remarks discourage his path to excellence. He not only graduated from high school, but went on to graduate from college (and in 4 years!), to top that off he had a job in his field waiting for him upon graduation.

Well, life was good until a cold day in February 2011. That day, the echoes of "the talk" rang in his ears. He was assaulted by a group of men he thought were gang members, who turned out to be NYC undercover policemen. It was a life altering ordeal from him. He was later told he matched the profile of a suspect (tall, black man in Brooklyn... go figure). He was in his own neighborhood, minding his own business and it was only 7 o'clock in the evening. I thank God every day that he is alive to give his testimony and that I had the insightfulness to give him "the talk" at an early age.

Proverbs 22:6 (KJV)
Train up a child in the way he should go: and when he is old, he will not depart from it.

The Condition: We as parents must prepare our children for their lives ahead.

The Promise: Our children will remember what we have taught them.

Web Post Bed-Stuy Patch, February 2011:

I realize that cops have a tough job, and I as a law abiding citizen, appreciate what they do. But there are good cops, and there are bad cops, and neither is above the law. If only these officers had identified themselves as police officers, this whole incident could have been avoided. You see, I have known Kam for 28 years, since the day he was born. I am his mother. Kameron is a law abiding, productive citizen (holy crap, he just was on jury duty last month.) He has NEVER gotten into any trouble, not as a child, not as a teen, and not as an adult. He is a taxpayer, a college graduate, and he has worked since he was 16 years old. Therefore, he should be able to walk down on his own street at 7:30 in the evening without worrying about being assaulted by those who we pay to protect and to serve. I thank God for protecting my child, because I do realize it could have been worse; and I pray for those parents whose outcome was not as fortunate as mine. No citizen should have to endure unwarrantable abusive treatment. There is no place for this in our society, and this abuse of power needs to stop.

P. WALKER-WILLIAMS

Secret Snow

Today in Houston, we had snow
And just what does this mean?
The people trip
The traffic's slow
It's really quite a scene.

To see the crystal flakes of snow
As each one drifts along.
The children rush
Before it's gone
They know it won't last long.

People at their windows
Standing there amazed
Looking up
And all around
As if they're in a daze.

Tomorrow we'll have sunshine
And one would never know
That what we had today
Was melted secret snow.

SECRET SNOW

Job 37:6 (NIV)
He says to the snow, 'Fall on the earth,' and to the rain shower, 'Be a mighty downpour.'

It is a rare occasion in Houston when we have snow, and we tend to celebrate it. Ironically, I was born in Chicago, one of the coldest places I know, where snow was a fairly common occurrence. I grew up in Memphis, so again, snow is very common. But in Houston, shoot, it is a rare occasion. In the more than 30 years since I have lived here I can count the times we have had snow on one hand.

This is a light-hearted poem, which celebrates God's goodness in everything.

Genesis, 1:31 (NIV)
God saw all that he had made, and it was good.

Fact: Everything the Lord has made is good.

P. WALKER-WILLIAMS

Economic Bondage

Not enough hours in each day
Rise before dawn then off on my way

Driving to work, I remember to pray
Thank you Lord is what I say

Time passes by, all work no play
Eight hours gone, I've earned my pay

Rip and run, do what I may
Sun's gone down, but that's O.K.

Shower, shampoo, then hit the hay
Whisper a prayer before I lay

Not enough hours in each day

ECONOMIC BONDAGE

Isaiah 43:16 (NIV)
This is what the LORD says-- he who made a way through the sea, a path through the mighty waters.

Sometimes it seems like we just can't catch up. We can't catch up with rest, we can't catch up with our bills, and we can't catch up with life. It is so easy to get weary. The millennials are all about "work-life balance" – which is a beautiful thing. But they should be mindful that someone paved the way for them to achieve this luxury. Many parents have worked long hard hours in order for their children to thrive and to make ends meet.

Psalm 118:5 (NIV)
In my anguish I cried to the Lord, and he answered by setting me free.

High Tech and High Heels Blog Post:
Friday, March 31, 2006

Today, I am having "one of those days." You know, the kind of day, that makes you wonder is it all worth it. My Mother taught me to work hard and have a good work ethic, and I would be rewarded, prosper and do well. Events that have taken place at my "day job" this past month has caused me to wonder, is that really true?

I decided to do, what I do, when I am having "one of those days,"

... I cried to the Lord for help.

Just like that, I got my answer! The words of one of my favorite hymns came to me crystal clear, this gave me a second wind, a glimmer of hope.

THE LORD WILL MAKE A WAY SOMEHOW!

P. WALKER-WILLIAMS

Women of the Cross

We come from separate walks of life
To learn about God's word.
Each one chose you to guide us
Through some message that we heard.

We are women…
Who have joined together to glorify our Lord.
Women who are faithful, and all on one accord.

We thank you for your leadership,
For your prayers and for your trust.
Thankful for "those ties that bind
Our hearts in Christian love."

We are women…
Like those who stayed near the cross when the disciples fled.

Women

First to witness the resurrection of Jesus
from the dead.

And in appreciation
For all the work you do
We thank God for the blessing
Of leading us to you.

We are women...
Like Naomi and Ruth,
bound one to the other
Women
Making God the center of our lives, and
caring for one another.

We thank you for your teachings
Spreading hope to those thought loss.
We thank you for the love you've shown
The Women of the Cross.

WOMEN OF THE CROSS

Acts 1:14 (KJV)
These all continued with one accord in prayer and supplication, with the women, and Mary, the mother of Jesus, and with his brethren.

In 1994, the women's ministry at my church (Bay Area Baptist, Houston, TX) asked me to write a poem for Pastor's appreciation day. I wanted to write a poem that not only thanked our pastor for his leadership, but was tied to the importance of women in the bible.

Women are often treated as second-class citizens not only in third world countries, but also here in the US. We are often discriminated against not only in the workplace but in many places of worship. I remember, as a child, women not being able to stand in the pulpit or being able to wear pants in the sanctuary. As a young adult, I was even asked by some elderly church women to leave the church because I came to choir practice (after work) and happened to have on pants. (FYI, I was not having that! I immediately went to the pastor's office in protest, and to my surprise he agreed with me.)

Although we as women have come a long way, we still have a long way to go. We still do not get equal pay at work, and we still suffer domestic abuse and rape. We must empower our young girls.

Proverbs 31:25 (KJV)
Strength and honor are her clothing; she shall rejoice in time to come.

We must teach them that women have not only played an important role in world history, but it is documented in the Bible. But did you know that there are 188 women mentioned by name in the Bible; and hundreds more women in the bible that are unnamed? Some of these women were great leaders like Deborah in the book of Judges 4.4; queens like the Queen of Sheba, (1 Kings 10:13); prophets like Anna (Luke 2:36) and the faithful like Ruth who has an entire book named after her in the Old Testament.

But the women who touch my heart the most are the women who stood by Jesus at the cross. Even when the disciples fled, these women stood witness and were faithful to the end.

John 19:25 (KJV)

Now there stood by the cross of Jesus his mother, and his mother's sister, Mary the wife of Cleophas, and Mary Magdalene.

Matthew 27:55-66 (NIV)

Many women were there, watching from a distance. They had followed Jesus from Galilee to care for his needs. Among them were Mary Magdalene, Mary the mother of James and Joseph, and the mother of Zebedee's sons.

P. WALKER-WILLIAMS

The Call

You have conquered many obstacles
And all in God's name
So now you've been called…
Can you handle the strain?

For people will talk
Some will snicker and sneer
Some will have doubts
While others will fear.

Keep lifting Christ up,
Just stand on His word
Keep praising His name
And you will be heard.

We've witnessed your actions
Compassion and love,
You are filled with His spirit,
And washed in His blood.

We are all on your side
In each of your goals
We have seen in your eyes
God's call on your soul.

A fisher of men…
Well now is the hour
To bring forth the message
Of God's divine power.

THE CALL

Matthew 22:14 (KJV)
For many are called, but few are chosen.

When God puts a call on your heart, it is up to you to answer that call. You may be called to preach God's word, you may be called to sing, you may be called to be a doctor, and there are many callings. Some people fight their callings, but when God chooses you, your soul will not rest until you submit and answer God's call, no matter what it is.

Just because you like to do something, does not mean that is what you were called to do. I like to sing, but I would be broke as a dog if I tried to do it for a living, because I know that is not what God called me to do. In this same way, there are people who preach the gospel that are false prophets, my mama says "they were not called, they just went." After all, saving souls can be a profitable business.

It is up to each individual to choose a spiritual leader that interprets God's word in a way that it feeds their soul. Someone you respect as an individual, and who walks in the light. Everyone is different. You might receive the word best when it is presented calmly or you might respond better to the word delivered through a little whooping and shouting. What is best for you might be horrible for someone else and vice versa. You have the option to choose a pastor you trust with your spiritual growth.

If God has put a calling on your life, you can rely on God's promise in the book of Matthew:

Matthew 4:19 (KJV)
And he saith unto them, "Follow me, and I will make you fishers of men."

The Condition: Follow Christ.

The Promise: He will make you a fisher of men.

Unto Others

I might not call you every day
Or even once a week,
But the test of a true friend
Is not how much you speak.

A friend is that someone who cares
And often thinks of you
Someone you might not see for months
But welcome when you do.

Allow me space to make mistakes
And don't take them to heart.
Allow me time to grow and learn
If we spend time apart.

Lord knows that I'm not perfect,
I hope that you do, too.
Consider this when you find fault
In little things I do.

Time is the magic element
In passing friendship's test.
For it stands still and waits for you
When friendship is at its best.

UNTO OTHERS

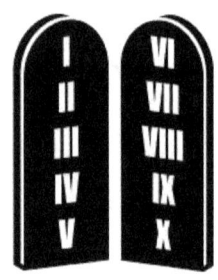

Luke 6:31 (NIV)
Do to others as you would have them do to you.

There are many different types of friends and levels of friendships; those from childhood, college, work, neighborhood, and church. Shoot, I have friends I have met at the bus stop.

You meet people continually though your life and as you meet more people, your circle of friends continues to grow. Some of your friends remain in your life forever, while other friends are in your life during a specific time.

Growing up, my friend Debra called me the "friend of the friendless", because I tended to befriend everyone. However, the older I got I realized that friendships change. Sometimes people grow apart or are simply separated by distance or time.

Unfortunately, some friendships can become toxic; full of jealously, competitiveness or broken promises.

In these cases, it may be time to step away, just to keep from saying or doing anything you may regret later.

Proverbs 13:20 (KJV)
He that walketh with wise men shall be wise: but a companion of fools shall be destroyed.

The Condition: We must keep good company.

The Promise: If not, we may be brought to ruin.

The sign of a true friendship is a bond that isn't altered by time, distance, or personal growth.

Proverbs 17:17 (NIV)
A friend loves at all times…

P. WALKER-WILLIAMS

Letting Go

The baggage I carry is full of hurt
A broken heart
And bits of dirt.
Memories of things gone bad
Sorrow, tears
A life that's sad.

Just want to lay these burdens down.
Forget the past
And touch the ground
Let my life
Begin anew
But this I don't know how to do.

Something new each day revealed
Some things false,
Yet others real.

Stirring memories... I have a lot
Of things forgiven
But not forgot.

Just how do you ease the pain?
When life goes on
But tears remain.

The grace of God
Helped get me through
But life's still hard
So I share with you
My pain,
My sorrow,
And, yes, my hurt.
The memories mixed in the dirt.

LETTING GO

Psalm 147:3 (NIV)
He heals the brokenhearted and binds up their wounds.

Breakups happen; and when they do, this can be an agonizing time. The aftermath of broken relations can include self-doubt, casting fault, and broken hearts. During this time, you may feel like your world is coming to an end. Trust me, I understand that at this time there is nothing your family and friends can tell you that will make you feel any better. It takes time.

But you need to know that you are not alone. You are not the first person, nor will you be the last to have a broken heart. You are in good company, we have all been there. I know, I know… this does not make it any easier, but just as we have made it through, so will you.

So, what encouragement does the Lord have for you during this time?

Isaiah 41:10 (NIV)

So do not fear, for I am with you; do not be dismayed, for I am your God. I will strengthen you and help you; I will uphold you with my righteous right hand.

The Promise: God's got you. He will get you through this.

Dream Dancer

A little girl
Up on her toes
A secret dream
That just she knows.

She jumps and leaps
All through the air,
She practices hard, rehearses with care.
An arabesque,
A split, a turn.
So much more
She has to learn.

A pirouette
Then kick, now bow.
So many steps to learn
But how?

The curtain opens
The light comes on.
Glitter, glitz...
Time to perform.

Like poetry in motion,
She captivates the crowd.
Bravo! More!
They cheer out loud.

Not long ago, she was just a child.
But time went by,
And crowds went wild.

The little girl that once did prance
Dream was fulfilled...
She grew to dance.

DREAM DANCER

Ecclesiastes 3:4 (KJV)
… A time to weep and a time to laugh, a time to mourn and a time to dance.

I don't remember a time in my life when I didn't love to dance. If there was music playing, I was dancing. If not on the floor, in my seat or in my head. I come from a dancing family. My mother loves to dance, so did all her sisters, my cousins, and my home girls! (My dad, not so much, but he was known to bob his head while he tapped his foot.)

The first 8mm recording of me is of me doing the twist on top of the washing machine. And whenever there was a grown-up family gathering, the only time the children were allowed to participate was to come show the adults how to do the latest dances. So, it is no wonder as a child I dreamed of being a dancer.

In grade school I took dancing lessons at neighborhood community centers; in Jr. High and High School I was mentored by some great dance instructors and choreographers; in college I took every dance class that was offered at the

University of Memphis (and got all A's). I taught neighborhood children in Memphis (Alcy Youth Club); praise dancers at church (Bay Area Baptist); and owned and taught at my dance studio (Hip Bones in Motion).

Psalm 149:3 (NIV)
Let them praise His name with dancing and make music to him with timbrel and harp.

So, although I didn't follow my dream to become a professional dancer, my dream was fulfilled by teaching others to dance. In Jeremiah 31 after God declares he will make them a happy nation once again. The people celebrate with dance and God gives them an unconditional promise to give them comfort and joy!

Jeremiah 31:13 (NIV)
Then young women will dance and be glad, young men and old as well. I will turn their mourning into gladness; I will give them comfort and joy instead of sorrow.

The Passing of Youth

It is such a wonder
How we each evolve.
Savoring life's moments
With each problem solved.

With youth life was so simple
To dream, to hope, to feel
No responsibilities,
No job and, yes, no bills.

With youth life held true vision
Of prophecies revealed
Tomorrow took forever
Each moment hung
So still.

With youth life was eternal
Days just drifted by
Life would last forever
Mortality a lie.

With youth time passed so slowly
Yet, wisdom did unfold
Knowledge seeped into our minds
A sign of growing old.

As we witness all life's miracles
That are part of the Master's plan
The older we get,
The more we know,
The less we understand.

THE PASSING OF YOUTH

2 Corinthians 4:16 (NIV)
Therefore we do not lose heart. Though outwardly we are wasting away, yet inwardly we are being renewed day by day.

Aging is a natural part of life. To be alive means you grow older, that is just the way it is. The bible tells us that although our body ages, our soul is renewed day by day. Just think about it, your soul is as new as the day you were born!

I have always wanted to age graciously, but I remember when I turned 30, Oh, My Goodness! I thought I was old as water! Now looking back I have to laugh, and that was a half-a-lifetime ago. I wrote "The Passing of Youth" when I was in my 40's, now as I approach 60 here is a look back...

Passing of Youth Addendum

Turned 40, Woke up sane
Still in my right mind, there was no pain.

No new wrinkles, no gray hair
Still got my vision, still got my flair.

Turned 50, I thought it was chic,
Body still working, although it's weak

Still no wrinkles, hair still black
Bones don't ache, joints don't crack.

60's approaching, a few gray hairs
Vision's worse, but who cares.

Gain a few pounds, bones sometimes ache.
God continues to bless me, so life is great.

Isaiah 46:4 (NIV)
Even to your old age and gray hairs I am he, I am he who will sustain you. I have made you and I will carry you; I will sustain you and I will rescue you.

God's unconditional promise: God will sustain me.

Sense Me

What do you see
when you see my face?
Can you see my inner beauty?
Or do you just see race?

What do you feel
when you look in my eyes?
Do you experience my struggle?
Can you hear my ancestor's cries?

What do you hear
when you call my name?
Is it too ethnic for you?
Or is it just too plain?

What do you feel
when you touch my hand?
Do you remember my passage?
To this strange new land?

What do you smell
when you long for me?
Do you remember the ocean?
Can you smell the sea?

What do you taste
when your lips touch mine?
Do you think we are different?
Or are we two of a kind?

You must accept my depth
to truly love me.
You must know my journey,
It is more than you just see.

From the Middle Passage,
to the election of Barack.
Sense my many layers as virtues,
And not as stumbling blocks.

SENSE ME

Proverbs 20:12 (NIV)
Ears that hear and eyes that see-- the LORD has made them both.

Sight. Hearing. Touch. Smell. Taste.

These senses contribute to our preception of the world around us.

I wrote this poem from the perspective of an African American contemplating entering into a relationship with someone of a different race or culture. I thought of what questions I would ask to establish a foundation based on truth and trust. I bring with me the middle passage and the history of my enslaved people.

There have always been and always will be racists. Those you have already determined their opinions without any merit. But people have been mixing since biblical times; and I, like most African Americans, do not have to go back too many generations in order to find a white ancestor (or two) in our family tree.

Some of this lineage can be painful. As many of

our matriarchal ancestors had no choice in who fathered their children. But some of the lineage is beautiful and based on choice and true love which saw no color.

1 Corinthians 13:7 (NIV) speaks of Love:
It always protects, always trusts, always hopes, always perseveres.

Mixed-relationships are more in the open now than when I was growing up. Resulting in families that can blend the best of all cultures. However, we should not forget our past. It is a part of us, it makes us who we are.

Galatians 3:28 (NIV)
There is neither Jew nor Gentile, neither slave nor free, nor is there male and female, for you are all one in Christ Jesus.

A Silenced Woof

Someone I love has gone away
Yet, I still live to face another day.
Memories clinging consuming my soul
Of thoughts and smells... an empty bowl.

Someone I love is no longer here
To share a smile
Or linger near.
To lick my face, or catch a ball
To sit and stay, to hear me call.

Someone I love at last is free
To walk unleashed, to pee on trees.
To run for miles, to jump and play
Someone I love has gone away.

A SILENCED WOOF

Job 12:10 (NIV)
In His hand is the life of every creature and the breath of all mankind.

Pets can be faithful companions. They tend to love their owners unconditionally and give us much joy. I am, and have always been, a pet lover. I especially love dogs and cats and, growing up, I had my share of each.

The love of animals is a trait I apparently passed on to my son. When he was a little boy he told me that when he grew up, he wanted to be either a veterinarian or join the circus, LOL! Well, although he decided against both, he is now the parent to both a dog (Ms. Yoyo) and a cat (Mr. Trips).

One of our family pets was named Tyson (yep, after Mike) and he was poisoned by some neighborhood children and died in 1996. This poem is a tribute to our much loved pet.

So, what does the Bible say about pets and animals? Well, we all know they must be important because they are mentioned in the Bible from Genesis to Revelations. Here are a few scriptures to reflect upon:

Genesis 1:21 (NIV)
So God created the great creatures of the sea and every living thing with which the water teems and that moves about in it, according to their kinds, and every winged bird according to its kind. And God saw that it was good.

Revelation 5:13 (NIV)
Then I heard every creature in heaven and on earth and under the earth and on the sea, and all that is in them, saying:

"To him who sits on the throne and to the Lamb be praise and honor and glory and power, for ever and ever!"

P. WALKER-WILLIAMS

The Gift of Thanks

Life is a journey
We are blessed to go through
Full of love and blessings
And one of them is you.

We are so thankful
For our family and friends
Grateful for just knowing
On you we can depend.

We are also thankful
For all the memories we share
So, we take this time to tell you
Just how much we care.

THE GIFT OF THANKS

1 Corinthians 1:4 (NIV)
I always thank my God for you because of His grace given you in Christ Jesus.

Thank you. These two simple words have a wealth of meaning. In both giving thanks to God, but also thanking one another. My girlfriends and I have discussed how some people (not all) in the younger generations no longer send thank you cards. Instead they may get a phone call, but more likely an email or text. I cannot tell you how many wedding gifts I have given and never heard a word back. So in the back of my mind I am wondering "Did they get it?" You kind of hate to ask them about it, but you want to make sure it wasn't lost in the mail or stolen from an envelope at the wedding (gift cards or cash).

All of this boils down to good manners. My mother always told me that "please and thank you" were magic words. That is a lesson that has stayed with me my entire lifetime. I know that life can get hectic, but sometimes instead of a text, pick up the phone and tell someone hello.
Instead of an email, send a hand-written card.

I will tell you a secret, if you have ever sent me a birthday card... every year... most likely, I still have it. It is tangible. It is something I can hold and think about you. I also keep all personalized Christmas cards, you know the one with family photos, etc. Call me a pack rat if you will, but I appreciate anyone who thinks enough of me to let me know.

Lastly, a reminder to the young parents out there. Teach your kids to not only say thanks, but send a handwritten note sometimes. We grandparents, aunties, and uncles really cherish these memories.

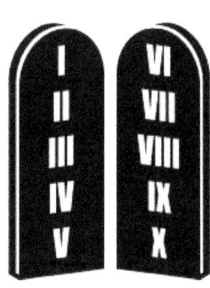

1 Thessalonians 5:11
Therefore, encourage one another and build each other up, just as in fact you are doing.

P. WALKER-WILLIAMS

Bandwagon

I can't jump on your bandwagon,
I have a wagon of my own.
My own opinions, my own thoughts,
In my own secluded zone.

Why spend my time cutting people down?
I'd rather lift them up.
Hate tears away my goodness,
And eats away my soul.

We all have dreams, though some deferred,
No one's better than another's.
Don't get caught up in the devil's lie,
Stand up for all your brothers.

Divide and conquer is Satan's game,
Don't let him draw you in.
He has lots of practice at his craft
And you could never win.

Have your own thoughts,
stop following fools
And stand upon God's word.
Keep prayed up, stay in the light,
And your prayers will be heard.

BANDWAGON

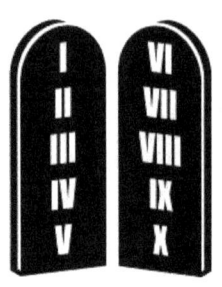

Colossians 4:6 (NIV)
Let your conversation be always full of grace, seasoned with salt, so that you may know how to answer everyone.

Social media has given everyone a platform. Things that individuals would be reluctant to say to a person's face comes very easy when one is hidden behind a screen. I have seen some very hurtful things said about a lot of people. I was online today and was appalled at some of the ugly things I saw being said about real people. I have to remind myself not to get caught up in the frenzy. Of course, I comment on TV shows like anyone else, but I make it a point to step back before I post and ask myself, "Is what I am posting mean-spirited?" Sometimes, it might be, because I am human and I can cut-up with the best of them. But I am a work in progress and trying to be a better person. I don't want to be just another person jumping on someone else's bandwagon.

For situations when we might succumb to peer pressure, God gives us these instructions:

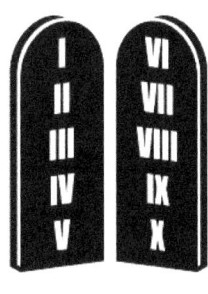

Exodus 23:2 (NIV)

Do not follow the crowd in doing wrong. When you give testimony in a lawsuit, do not pervert justice by siding with the crowd.

Proverbs 4:14-15(NIV)

Do not set foot on the path of the wicked or walk in the way of evildoers. Avoid it, do not travel on it; turn from it and go on your way.

P. WALKER-WILLIAMS

Coming Down the Mountain

As the polls closed,
the world stood watch
Electoral votes counted.
I whispered a prayer,
I closed my eyes,
As anticipation mounted.

I was holding my breath
when the phone rang,
My son said "they're about to call it."
270 was needed and had been reached
so they finally announced it.

My dad transitioned a week before
the presidential inauguration.
He didn't live to see the day
a black man became
the leader of our nation.

In my father's stead I stood proud
Excited to breathe this day!
To witness change, to overcome
To see a way made from no way.

Dr. King made it to this mountain top
He saw this Promised Land.
Although he didn't make it with us
At least now we understand.

As we come down the mountain,
There may be difficult days ahead.
But we thank God for Martin's vision
And prophesying
"Yes we can!"

COMING DOWN THE MOUNTAIN

Hebrews 11:1 (KJV)
Now faith is the substance of things hoped for, the evidence of things not seen.

I am not a very political person. I try to stay informed and I vote. That about sums it up. I am a card toting Democrat. That is my party of choice and I respect the fact that some people choose differently. Thus we have a democratic republic.

I have said all of that to say this… It is not my intent to offend anyone with my personal political beliefs. I voted for President Obama, and I am still glad I did. I wrote the following blog post the day after he won his first presidential election. It expressed how I felt on that very special day in America's History.

Matthew 17:20 (NIV)
He replied, "Because you have so little faith. Truly I tell you, if you have faith as small as a mustard seed, you can say to this mountain, 'Move from here to there,' and it will move. Nothing will be impossible for you.

P. WALKER-WILLIAMS

High Tech and High Heels Blog Post:
"Faith versus Hope"
January 2009

This week I witnessed something that I honestly never thought I would see in my lifetime, an African American become president of the United States. Surely I hoped for it, I dreamed about it and I prayed on it. But, what I lacked was faith. That was until Barack Obama.

Of course, I supported him from the onset. He was intelligent, articulate, charismatic, and wholesome, he had something special, something I had not ever seen in a president, and something that reminded me a lot of Martin Luther King – the ability to bring people together.

I was born in Chicago in the fifties and I grew up in Memphis in the sixties/seventies. My mother was very active in the Civil Rights Movement, and she always had me in tow. I marched with Dr. King in Memphis, and heard him speak at Mason Temple. Although, I really didn't understand everything that was going on, I knew he was special. I could see it in my mother's eyes, I could hear it in his voice, and I could feel it in my heart. We had great hope for the future and in Dr. King's dream. Regrettably, his dream was deferred, and we would have to wait 30 years to see it come into fruition.

"But I want you to know tonight, that we, as a people will get to the Promised Land." - Martin Luther King, Jr. (April 1968)

In 1976, when I was finally eligible to vote in a presidential election, I voted for Jimmy Carter. It was a proud day for me. I later went on to vote for Carter again, Mondale, Clinton and Gore.

After the Florida fiasco in 2000, when my fellow Texan, George W. Bush, won the election, I lost my faith not only in the system, but also in our country. I was thinking, "Here we are in a new millennium, and my people are still being treated with disrespect and discrimination." I thought that my country was surely better than this, it not only made me sad but it hurt. It hurt me to my heart.

2004 would be the first time my son would be eligible to vote in a presidential election, and I was just as excited that day as I was on his first day of school. Unfortunately, he wouldn't let me take pictures, but it was a great day, nevertheless. I was so proud of him, and he was so excited. He, my husband, and I cast our votes for Kerry. We were all disappointed when George W. won again. I was especially disappointed because this was my son's first experience. I didn't want him to give up on the system.

Our youth came out in record numbers that year. I could sense the beginning of change.

I was watching Oprah one day and she had Senator Barack Obama on her show. We all remembered him from the 2004 Democratic Convention. That was the first time I realized that he might truly consider running for president. I, like Oprah, hoped he would. I argued with many people, mostly black folks, during the beginning. A common thread of conversation was "You know this country is not ready for a Black President." Well, I beg to differ, and as my mother would say "Pam, you know you will argue with God." And that is when I realized, I had F-A-I-T-H! I had Faith, not just hope, that this man, Barack Obama, was an instrument of change. He was more than qualified, and he was what our country needed – right now.

My family (mother, husband, and son) are ALL proud supporters of Barack Obama (cousins, friends, co-workers, too.) While we chanted "Yes, We Can!" and "Fired Up and Ready to Go!" we witnessed our country change. It wasn't just Black people supporting Obama; it was people of all races, ages, religions, nationalities, and even folks in other countries.

Through the primaries, the caucus (which I hope I NEVER have to do again), the democratic convention, the election, and finally the inauguration, I have been proud.

I have been Proud of my ancestors, proud of my family, and proud of my country.

I now have not only hope but faith for our future.

What a wonderful time to be alive! God Bless President Obama and God Bless America!

P. WALKER-WILLIAMS

Ancestor Unknown

So many died to give us freedom.
Yet, they were never free.
So many marched to give us liberty
A life they didn't live to see.

So many toiled and worked in the fields
To keep their children fed.
So many rose early to raise other's kids,
While their own kids still laid in bed.

So many washed, scrubbed, and cleaned
Other people's homes.
So many cried just at the thought
Of leaving their families all alone.

So many brought their children to church
To listen to God's word.

So many rejoiced, while lifting their hands to shout
In hopes that their prayers would be heard.

So many juggled while working two jobs
To pay their child's tuition.
So many glowed and beamed with pride
When their dreams came to fruition.

So many of our ancestors sacrificed,
Yet, we don't know their names.
To them we give abundant thanks.
Their victory is claimed.

ANCESTOR UNKNOWN

Zephaniah 3:19-20 (NIV)
At that time I will deal with all who oppressed you. I will rescue the lame; I will gather the exiles. I will give them praise and honor in every land where they have suffered shame.

At that time I will gather you; at that time I will bring you home. I will give you honor and praise among all the peoples of the earth when I restore your fortunes before your very eyes," says the Lord.

I wrote "Ancestor Unknown" as a result of a blog post I wrote in 2012, titled "I Speak your Name." The post honored the memory of all of my family and friends who had passed on at that time. While I was revising this book, I kept thinking about all of the ancestors whose names I do not know. These unknown ancestors are just as much a part of me. So many gave up their lives for my freedom, and this poem is my way of speaking their names.

High Tech and High Heels Blog Post:
"I Speak Your Name"
Sunday, September 9, 2012

When I was young, it seemed to be a rare occasion for a friend to pass away. Of course, old people died, that was what they were supposed to do. But people my age... not so much. I lost my great-grandmother at the age of 5, my maternal grandmother at the age of 9, and my grandfather at the age of 10. Strange thing is that I remember each one's passing. I remember how sad my mother was, and I remember not fully understanding I would not see them again.

When I was in junior high, the unthinkable happened, one of my friends died. I am still not sure exactly what happened, but I remember her being in the hospital, and the next thing I remember is going to her funeral. Her name was Thea Jones. A few years later, I went to visit my friend, Jeanie, and there was a black wreath on the door. Her name was Jeanette Fisher, and she had passed from complications of Sickle Cell. We had been friends our whole childhood, and I never even knew she had the trait.

Then, it was on to college and the passing of my friend, Rodney, who we called "Bay Shay". The night before he died, he and his best friend, Andre, came to visit Paulette (my roommate) and me. We were in college, and considered them our little brothers. They were so excited because they were seniors in high school, and it wouldn't be long before their graduation. We fed them, and stayed up all night talking about nothing and everything. We literally had to put them out! The next day, Rodney and

Andre went to play basketball and Rodney passed out. He had a heart attack and died. He was only 17 years old. I will never forget it, I will never forget that phone call.

I only had one friend I knew that was born on the same day in the same year as me. His name was John Gunn. He was 6' 9", and a center for the Memphis State basketball team. John came down with what we thought was a cold, and it turned out to be a rare disease called Stevens-Johnson syndrome. John died on December 21, 1976. I couldn't believe it. He was not only my friend, but my exact same age. We were too young to die.

Years went by, and eventually, my aunts and uncles began to pass away. My mom's oldest sister Geraldine (who we called Sister) was the first. Her dying wasn't a surprise to me because she smoked a pack of Lucky Strike cigarettes (with no filter) each and every day. So, I wasn't in shock, but she was the first of that generation.

In 1986, the same week as the Space Shuttle Challenger disaster, my only brother was killed. The world as I knew it changed that day. How could my baby brother be dead? I just could not wrap my head around this. He had a one-year-old daughter, and a 1-week-old son. He was only 23 years old. His death devastated my mother, and she hasn't been the same since. She is like two people; my mom before my brother died, and my mom after my brother died. Strange, but true.

Since then, I have lost all of my aunts and uncles, my god-parents, my mother-in-law, father-in-law, a nephew, my father, and many friends.

In 2010, I lost one of my best friends, Karan. My world was forever changed, again. This week, I lost another friend, Patti. The circle of life continues. My ancestors believe if you speak the names of the dead, they will never truly die. They will live on forever...
Flora, Almetta, Edgar, Sadie, Eugene, Cora, John W., Thea, Jeannie, Rodney, John G., Sister, Terry, Cathy, Met, Lucille, Pap, Nan, Frazier, Tootum, Corbin, Ruth, Mallory, Stanley, Wendell, David, Reginald, Connie, Ethel, Bernice, Georgetta, Tracey, Karan, Maeon, Arnita, Carrie Mae, Joe Jr., Reevis, Reesha, Reaumel, Coochie, Jan, and Patti.

I speak your name, I speak your name.

Philippians 1:3 (NIV)
I thank my God every time I remember you.

A Dash of Soul

Families pass on traditions and love
From parents, relatives,
and ancestors above
Even though some are gone,
we still feel them near
By preparing these dishes
that they held so dear.

Holidays come and we start
planning the feast
Of cakes and pies and
rolls made with yeast
We laugh, we cry, we dance, we sing
We share the love tradition brings.

It is through these meals
we show we care
For our family and friends
with whom memories we share.

When preparing these meals
and reminiscing the old...
Add a pinch of love and a dash of soul.

A DASH OF SOUL

Ecclesiastes 9:7 (NIV)
Go, eat your food with gladness, and drink your wine with a joyful heart, for God has already approved what you do.

This poem is from a cookbook I compiled in 2014 named "A Dash of Soul". The cookbook contains recipes from my family and friends that I enjoyed growing up with in Memphis. A "Dash of Soul" was also the name of my mother's modeling troop in the 1970's. They toured local churches and night clubs with their entertaining fashion shows mixed with comedy and music. It was a special time in my childhood as are the memories of family gatherings and holidays.

The bible has many scriptures centered on feasts and celebrations. Family celebrations allow us to give thanks to God, fellowship with one another, and reminisce times gone by.

Proverbs 15:17 (NIV)
Better a small serving of vegetables with love than a fattened calf with hatred.

My Joy

My joy comes in the morning,
    when I wake and see your smile.

My joy comes after waking,
    when you hold me for a while.

My joy comes once I've risen,
    and we sit to talk and share.

My joy comes when we kiss goodbye,
    for I really know you care.

My joy comes each time I think of you,
    on and off throughout the day.

My joy comes upon returning home
    and I know that you're OK.

My joy comes when we discuss our day,
    and laugh about our sorrows.

My joy comes as we prepare for sleep,
    knowing that we share tomorrow.

MY JOY

Psalm 30:5 (KJV)
For His anger endureth but a moment; in His favour is life: weeping may endure for a night, but joy cometh in the morning.

I tend to wake up around 3:00 a.m. every morning. Sometimes, I get up, and other times I just lay there and try to go back to sleep. I choose to think that this is my personal time to commune with God. This is the time when I am most creative. I come up with solutions to software coding problems, I can remember where I left my keys, and I compose music and lyrics.

This morning as I was lying in bed, I looked at my husband (who, by the way, does not have any problems sleeping) and all I could do was smile. I though how blessed am I that God chose this man to be my mate; and through all the challenges we have faced, the fact that I am able to wake up next to him each day brings me pure joy.

In the words of one of my favorite songs, "I'd Rather" performed by Luther Vandross (written by Anthony Crawford) - *"I'd rather have bad times with you than good times with someone else."*

And from THE WORD –

1 Corinthians 13:13 (NIV)

And now these three remain: faith, hope and love. But the greatest of these is love.

The Broken Promise

I don't know where to begin.
The lies you told on our first date,
Or the lies told at the end.

You promised to protect me,
To be the shoulder where I could lean,
Instead you tried to hurt me,
How could you be so mean?

You promised that you'd love me,
Which was another lie.
Instead you flaunted your affairs,
Instead you made me cry.

You stood before God and made a vow,
You never meant to keep.
You broke my spirit and my heart,
All I could do was weep.

So many broken promises,
From such a broken man.
I pity you and who you are,
I just don't understand.

Our time is up, gave you my all.
I have prayed to God without ceasing,
For Him to help you find your way.
Now our promise I'm releasing.

THE BROKEN PROMISE

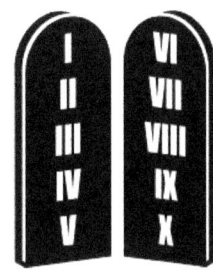

Ephesians 5:25 (KJV)
Husbands, love your wives, even as Christ also loved the church, and gave himself for it.

Between 2001 and 2012 the FBI domestic violence stats report that over 11,000 women were killed by their husbands or boyfriends. That is twice as many people that were killed in Afghanistan and Iraq during that same time period. These are some alarming statistics.

God does not want you to stay in an abusive relationship. This includes both physical and emotional violence.

Proverbs 10:6 (KJV)
Blessings are upon the head of the just: but violence covereth the mouth of the wicked.

I wrote this poem in the aftermath of a highly publicized domestic violence attack involving a professional football player and his wife. Every night on the news, they televised this attack over and over again. Of course, none of us know what goes on behind closed doors, but clearly they were having some problems. In this particular case, the couple chose to work things out, but that is not always the case.

I also lost a good friend in 2014 to domestic violence. She and I worked together, off and on, for 30 years. She was murdered by her husband. Relationships take work from both partners, and although God wants marriages to work, he does NOT want you to be abused. God has instructed your mate to love and protect you.

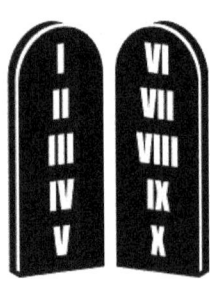

Malachi 2:16 (NIV)
"The man who hates and divorces his wife," says the Lord, the God of Israel, "does violence to the one he should protect, says the Lord Almighty." So be on your guard, and **do not be unfaithful.**

If you know your relationship is going in a bad direction, pray about it and seek counseling.

Thessalonians 5
Pray without ceasing.

If your mate has an unpredictable temper, threatens to hurt or kill you, or threatens to kill himself if you leave, it may be time for you to leave. If there is any physical violence to you or your children, **GET OUT OF THERE NOW!** Don't discuss it, don't give him any warning - sneak out like a thief in the night, your lives may depend on it. You can pray while you are leaving and raise holy hands once you are gone, but first, be safe.

Don't let your husband bible whip you with quotes about being submissive and obedient! The Bible has given him specific instructions (and even a commandment) on how he is supposed to treat you.

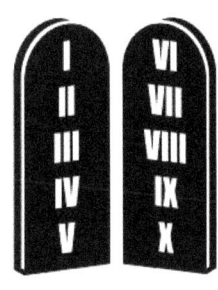

Colossians 3:19 (NIV)
Husbands, love your wives, and do not be harsh with them.

Exodus 20:2-17
Thou shalt not commit adultery.

Ephesians 5:25 (KJV)
Husbands, love your wives, even as Christ also loved the church, and gave himself for it;

Don't be ashamed to ask for help. Seek help from the police, clergy, family, or friends.

National Domestic Violence Hotline
1-800-799-7233 (SAFE)

Matthew 7:7 (NIV)
Ask and it will be given to you: seek and you will find: knock and the door will be opened to you. For everyone who asks received; he who seeks finds; and to him who knocks, the door will be opened.

Promise of a Rainbow

The Earth is filled with rainbows
Many splendors from above.
We must promise to protect it
We must fill the world with love.

We must cherish our surroundings
All the air and all the land.
There's no promise of tomorrow
The Earth's future is in our hands.

Take a stand for all the children
They deserve a place to grow.
So that they may see tomorrow
On an Earth filled with rainbows.

PROMISE OF A RAINBOW

Psalms 24:1-2
The earth is the LORD'S, and all it contains, the world, and those who dwell in it. For He has founded it upon the seas and established it upon the river.

In 1993, I wrote this poem in celebration of Earth Day, a day set aside in April for us to support causes to raise our consciousness about our environment.

When God created the world, it was truly a paradise. Just imagine, there was no pollution, the air was clean, the land was green, and the seas were all blue.

Years ago, when I visited Tulum in Mexico, I was taken aback at how beautiful and clear the water was. I cried when I saw the crystal blue water of the Caribbean Sea. I could imagine that was how all oceans looked when God created the world.

In 1994, I wrote a children's play using this poem along with God's promise in Genesis 9:13 and foundation to build on. Rainbows are metaphors that can symbolize so many things.

We can remember God's promise of a rainbow every time we see all the different hues of people, who, although have different skin tones, all are made of one blood.

Acts 17: 26
And hath made of one blood all nations of men for to dwell on all the face of the earth, and hath determined the times before appointed, and the bounds of their habitation.

We can remember God's promise of a rainbow every time we see all of the different colors in nature.

Ezekiel 28:13
You were in Eden, the garden of God; every precious stone adorned you: carnelian, chrysolite and emerald, topaz, onyx and jasper, lapis lazuli, turquoise and beryl. Your settings and mountings were made of gold; on the day you were created they were prepared.

God has given us all the precious gift of life. Although life is not always easy, God has given us a book filled with commandments, instructions, examples, facts, and promises that will help us get through the difficult times.

Whenever you are down, whenever you need faith, and whenever you need guidance, just search God's word and remember His unconditional promise of a rainbow.

Genesis 9:16 (NIV)

Whenever the rainbow appears in the clouds, I will see it and remember the everlasting covenant between God and all living creatures of every kind on the earth.

STUDY GUIDE

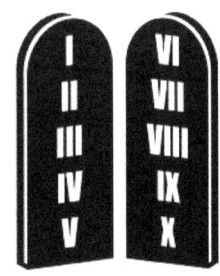

Commandments and Instructions

- Commandments - a divine rule or mandate given by God
- Instructions - directions

Facts and Examples

- Fact - something known to exist or to have happened in the past
- Examples (Parable) – a story that illustrates a spiritual or moral lesson

Praise and Prayer

- Praise - the offering of grateful admiration
- Prayer - a spiritual communion with God

Promises

Promise - a declaration that God will or will not do something in the future; it is unconditional and based on God's Grace

Covenants

Covenant - A solemn agreement made to humanity by God; a conditional agreement, contains a promise based on a fact or instruction

INDEX OF SCRIPTURES REFERENCES

Reference	Scripture	Poem
Genesis 1:21 (NIV)	So God created the great creatures of the sea and every living thing with which the water teems and that moves about in it, according to their kinds, and every winged bird according to its kind. And God saw that it was good.	A Silenced Woof
Genesis 1:31 (NIV)	God saw all that he had made, and it was good.	Secret Snow
Genesis 9:13 (NIV)	I have set my rainbow in the clouds, and it will be the sign of the covenant between me and the earth.	Promise of a Rainbow
Exodus 23:2 (NIV)	Do not follow the crowd in doing wrong. When you give testimony in a lawsuit, do not pervert justice by siding with the crowd.	Bandwagon
Job 12:10 (NIV)	In his hand is the life of every creature and the breath of all mankind.	A Silenced Woof
Job 37:6 (NIV)	He says to the snow, 'Fall on the earth,' and to the rain shower, 'Be a mighty downpour.'	Secret Snow

Reference	Scripture	Poem
Psalm 17:8 (NIV)	Keep me as the apple of the eye, hide me under the shadow of thy wings.	Shadows of Wings
Psalm 30:5 (KJV)	For his anger endureth but a moment; in his favour is life: weeping may endure for a night, but joy cometh in the morning.	My Joy
Psalm 91:11-12 (NIV)	For he will command his angels concerning you to guard you in all your ways; they will lift you up in their hands, so that you will not strike your foot against a stone.	Shadows of Wings
Psalm 118:5	In my anguish I cried to the Lord, and he answered by setting me free.	Economic Bondage
Psalm 147:3 (NIV)	He heals the brokenhearted and binds up their wounds.	Letting Go
Psalm 149:3 (NIV)	Let them praise his name with dancing and make music to him with timbrel and harp.	Dream Dancer
Proverbs 3:6 (KJV)	In all thy ways acknowledge Him and He shall direct thy paths.	Introduction

Reference	Scripture	Poem
Proverbs 4:14-15 (NIV)	Do not set foot on the path of the wicked or walk in the way of evildoers. Avoid it, do not travel on it; turn from it and go on your way.	Bandwagon
Proverbs 13:20 (KJV)	He that walketh with wise men shall be wise: but a companion of fools shall be destroyed.	Unto Others
Proverbs 15:17 (NIV)	Better a small serving of vegetables with love than a fattened calf with hatred.	A Dash of Soul
Proverbs 17:17 (NIV)	A friend loves at all times…	Unto Others
Proverbs 20:12 (NIV)	Ears that hear and eyes that see-- the LORD has made them both.	Sense Me
Proverbs 22:6 (KJV)	Train up a child in the way he should go: and when he is old, he will not depart from it.	I Sent My Child to School to Learn
Proverbs 31:25 (KJV)	Strength and honor are her clothing; She shall rejoice in time to come.	Women of the Cross
Ecclesiastes 3:4 (KJV)	A time to weep and a time to laugh, a time to mourn and a time to dance.	Dream Dancer
Ecclesiastes 9:7 (NIV)	Go, eat your food with gladness, and drink your wine with a joyful heart, for God has already approved what you do.	A Dash of Soul

Reference	Scripture	Poem
Isaiah 41:10 (NIV)	So do not fear, for I am with you; do not be dismayed, for I am your God. I will strengthen you and help you; I will uphold you with my righteous right hand.	Letting Go
Isaiah 43:16 (NIV)	This is what the LORD says-- he who made a way through the sea, a path through the mighty waters.	Economic Bondage
Isaiah 46:4 (NIV)	Even to your old age and gray hairs I am he, I am he who will sustain you. I have made you and I will carry you; I will sustain you and I will rescue you.	The Passing of Youth
Isaiah 54:17 (KJV)	No weapon that is formed against thee shall prosper; and every tongue that shall rise against thee in judgment thou shalt condemn…	I Sent my Child to School to Learn
Jeremiah 31:13 (NIV)	Then young women will dance and be glad, young men and old as well. I will turn their mourning into gladness; I will give them comfort and joy instead of sorrow.	Dream Dancer

Reference	Scripture	Poem
Zephaniah 3:19-20 (NIV)	At that time I will deal with all who oppressed you. I will rescue the lame; I will gather the exiles. I will give them praise and honor in every land where they have suffered shame. At that time I will gather you; at that time I will bring you home. I will give you honor and praise among all the peoples of the earth when I restore.	Ancestor Unknown
Malachi 2:16 (NIV)	The man who hates and divorces his wife," says the Lord, the God of Israel, "does violence to the one he should protect, says the Lord Almighty." So be on your guard, and do not be unfaithful.	The Broken Promise
Matthew 4:19 (KJV)	And he saith unto them, Follow me, and I will make you fishers of men.	The Call

Reference	Scripture	Poem
Matthew 6:6-7 (NIV)	But when you pray, go into your room, close the door and pray to your Father, who is unseen. Then your Father, who sees what is done in secret, will reward you. And when you pray, do not keep on babbling like pagans, for they think they will be heard because of their many words.	On My Knees
Matthew 17:20 (NIV)	He replied, "Because you have so little faith. Truly I tell you, if you have faith as small as a mustard seed, you can say to this mountain, 'Move from here to there,' and it will move. Nothing will be impossible for you.	Coming Down the Mountain
Matthew 22:14 (KJV)	For many are called, but few are chosen.	The Call
Matthew 27:55-56 (NIV)	Many women were there, watching from a distance. They had followed Jesus from Galilee to care for his needs. Among them were Mary Magdalene, Mary the mother of James and Joseph, and the mother of Zebedee's sons.	Women of the Cross

Reference	Scripture	Poem
Luke 6:31 (NIV)	Do to others as you would have them do to you.	Unto Others
John 19:25 (KJV)	Now there stood by the cross of Jesus his mother, and his mother's sister, Mary the wife of Cleophas, and Mary Magdalene.	Women of the Cross
Acts 1:14 (KJV)	These all continued with one accord in prayer and supplication, with the women, and Mary the mother of Jesus, and with his brethren	Women of the Cross
Romans 8:28 (KJV)	And we know that in all things God works for the good of those who love him, who have been called according to his purpose.	Introduction
1 Corinthians 1:4 (NIV)	I always thank my God for you because of his grace given you in Christ Jesus.	The Gift of Thanks
1 Corinthians 13:7 (NIV)	It always protects, always trusts, always hopes, always perseveres.	Sense Me
1 Corinthians 13:13 (NIV)	And now these three remain: faith, hope and love. But the greatest of these is love.	My Joy
2 Corinthians 4:16 (NIV)	Therefore we do not lose heart. Though outwardly we are wasting away, yet inwardly we are being renewed day by day	The Passing of Youth

Reference	Scripture	Poem
Galatians 3:28 (NIV)	There is neither Jew nor Gentile, neither slave nor free, nor is there male and female, for you are all one in Christ Jesus.	Sense Me
Philippians 1:3 (NIV)	I thank my God every time I remember you.	Ancestor Unknown
Colossians 4:6 (NIV)	Let your conversation be always full of grace, seasoned with salt, so that you may know how to answer everyone.	Bandwagon
1 Thessalonians 5:11 (NIV)	Therefore encourage one another and build each other up, just as in fact you are doing.	The Gift of Thanks
1 Timothy 2:8 (NIV)	Therefore I want the men everywhere to pray, lifting up holy hands without anger or disputing	On My Knees
Hebrews 11:1 (KJV)	Now faith is the substance of things hoped for, the evidence of things not seen.	Coming Down the Mountain
Hebrews 13:2 (NIV)	Do not forget to show hospitality to strangers, for by so doing some people have shown hospitality to angels without knowing it.	Shadows of Wings

Reference	Scripture	Poem
Revelation 5:13 (NIV)	Then I heard every creature in heaven and on earth and under the earth and on the sea, and all that is in them, saying: "To him who sits on the throne and to the Lamb be praise and honor and glory and power, for ever and ever!	Silenced Woof

AUTHOR'S NOTE

After I published "In a Heartbeat", my mother, Marian, reminded me of all the gazillion people in my life who I did not acknowledge. I have truly been blessed to have wonderful family and friends, and it was not my intent to leave anyone out. So here is the roll call, abundant thanks goes to:

My Family

My husband Ruffus, mother Marian, son Kameron, in-laws, aunts, uncles, cousins, nieces nephews, and godchildren! The Johnson, Thomas, Walker, Williams, Patterson, Harper, Sledge, and Savis families.

My Childhood Village

Alcy Road Neighborhood: The Harrison, Hunter, Pittman, Harris, Sargent, Johnson, Williams, Atkins, Webb, Young, Fields, Pritchard, and Bradley families.

Pentecostal M.B. Church: Especially my Sunday school teachers Mrs. Webb and Mrs. Woods.

All of my teachers and classmates:

Besty Ross Elementary (Chicago)
Mrs. Armstrong

Memphis City Schools

Walker Avenue - Mrs. Dorothy Dockery

Alcy Elementary - Mrs. Velma Pritchard

Corry Jr. High - Mrs. Bernice McClanahan &
Mrs. Allene McGuire

Booker T. Washington High School

The BTW Class of 1973

In Memory of

Mrs. Mary Nichols
Mrs. Lora Sandridge
Mrs. Catherine Johnson
Mr. Walter "Deke" Martin
Mrs. Norma Griffin

ACKNOWLEDGEMENTS

A Very Special Thank You goes to:

My Editors

Juanita Cole Towery
Xceptional Creations
(www.juanitacoletowery.see.me)

Jan Emanuel-Costley
Administrative Consulting Services
(www.adminconsulting.com)

My Sister-Cousins

Barbara, Geraldine, Caren, Mamie, and Wilma

My Sister-Friends

Debra, Wanda, Deon, Paulette, Eddgra, Jan, Mai, Juanita, Alona, Shelley, Tina, Pat, Mary, Jetola, Belinda, Vickie, and Nina

Sorors of Alpha Kappa Alpha Soritity, Inc.

My Good Book Club Sisters

Mary, Jetola, Shirley, Juanita, Pat, Yoni, Shermaine, and Shelley

My Family in Faith

Rev. Michael Satterfield, who is never too busy to stop and pray with me.

Rev. Cornelius and Yolanda Carrol (Abundant Love Christian Center), who always lift me up and make me feel abundantly loved.

Bishop Robert Lewis (Heritage Christian Acadamey), who stood in the gap when "I sent my child to school to learn."

My Literary Family

Bernice, Eric, Evelyn, Jewell, Kim, Nina, ReShonda, Stormy, Victor, and Victoria

The Page-Turner Network (pageturner.net)

Brown Girls Publishing

My SHE-roes

Alma, Monica (Dr. Moe), and Meghan

Everyone who purchased *"In a Heartbeat"*
(Especially those of you who posted pictures on Facebook: Andre, Elaine, Jan, Tina, Nina, Jetola, Paulette, Regina, Cheryl, Deb, Miranda, Jade, Eddgra, and Layla.)

ABOUT THE AUTHOR

Pamela Walker-Williams was born in Chicago, IL but moved to Memphis, TN at an early age. After college, she moved to Houston where she married, had one son, and worked at NASA Johnson Space Center for over 20 years.

Pam is a member of Alpha Kappa Alpha Sorority, Inc., and holds a Bachelor's Degree in Communication and a Master's Degree in Digital Media. Currently, she owns and operates "The Page-Turner Network" a web-design and digital media company.

Pam resides in the Houston, Texas area with her husband Ruffus *(who, by the way, is the luckiest man in the world.)*

Lagniappe

(A little something extra)

An Innocence Dies Still

I care not, whose life I take
Whose nectar I drain out.
I'll lie dormant as I wait.
No warning I'm about.

I need not even know your name
Or if you're man or child.
Your lifestyle won't influence my claim.
I watch, I wait, I smile.

You can make it easy
For me to do my job.
By making foolish choices
Your world you'll help me rob.

I know that you all wonder
Just how I came about.
For not race, nor sex, nor even age,
Is how I seek you out.

Many names I am called
By ignorance, hate and fear.
And yes, I'll answer to them all.
I'm AIDS and I am near.

AN INNOCENCE DIES STILL

1 Samuel 12: 22-23 (NIV)

For the sake of his great name the LORD will not reject his people, because the LORD was pleased to make you his own. As for me, far be it from me that I should sin against the LORD by failing to pray for you. And I will teach you the way that is good and right.

I wrote this poem on December 6, 1993, when the AIDS* epidemic was prominent in the news. Magic Johnson had announced he had HIV, Congress banned HIV infected people from entering the US, and by 1993 AIDS was the fourth leading cause of death among women aged 24-44 years in the US. This poem was included in the original publication of *"Promises Kept and Broken"*, however since we don't hear much about AIDS in the news anymore, I decided not to include it in this edition.

While having a conversation with one of my editors, Jan Emanuel-Costley, I told her why I decided not to include this poem. She brought it to my attention that this poem is not only relevant to AIDS, but other diseases such as breast cancer and Lupus. So during the final, final, final edit we decided to put the poem back in as "a little something extra". Jan reminded me that we never know what words are meant to encourage others, and this poem may have someone that it is meant to reach.

We all know someone who has been affected by disease. Let us lift each other in prayer, and have faith that God has the power to heal every disease and sickness.

Matthew 10:1 (NIV)

Jesus called his twelve disciples to him and gave them authority to drive out impure spirits and to heal every disease and sickness.

In the words of one of my favorite songs *Be Blessed* by Bishop Paul S. Morton...

"You can can depend on God
to see you through.
You can depend on me to pray for you."

Be Blessed.

*Acquired Immune Deficiency Syndrome (AIDS) is a disease which attacks the body's immune system, making it ineffective in fighting infections.

www.ingramcontent.com/pod-product-compliance
Lightning Source LLC
Chambersburg PA
CBHW061444040426
42450CB00007B/1212